I0813850

THE LITTLE BOOK OF THE

USA

First published in 2026 by OH
An Imprint of HEADLINE PUBLISHING GROUP LIMITED

1

Disclaimer:
All trademarks, copyright, quotations, company names, registered names, products, characters, logos and catchphrases used or cited in this book are the property of their respective owners.

Cataloguing in Publication Data is available from the British Library

ISBN 978-1-03543-485-5

Compiled and written by Malcolm Croft
Editorial: Stella Caldwell
Designed and typeset in Joanna Nova by Stephen Cary
Project manager: Russell Porter
Production: Marion Storz
Printed and bound in Dubai

Headline's policy is to use papers that are natural, renewable and recyclable products and made from woo grown in well-managed forests and other controlled sources. The logging and manufacturing processes are expected to conform to the environmental regulations c the country of origin.

HEADLINE PUBLISHING GROUP LIMITED
An Hachette UK Company
Carmelite House, 50 Victoria Embankment, London EC4Y 0DZ

The authorised representative in the EEA is Hachette Ireland, 8 Castlecourt Centre, Dublin 15, D15 XTP3, Ireland (email: info@hbgi.ie)

www.headline.co.uk www.hachette.co.uk

THE LITTLE BOOK OF THE

USA

AMERICA, THE BEAUTIFUL

CONTENTS

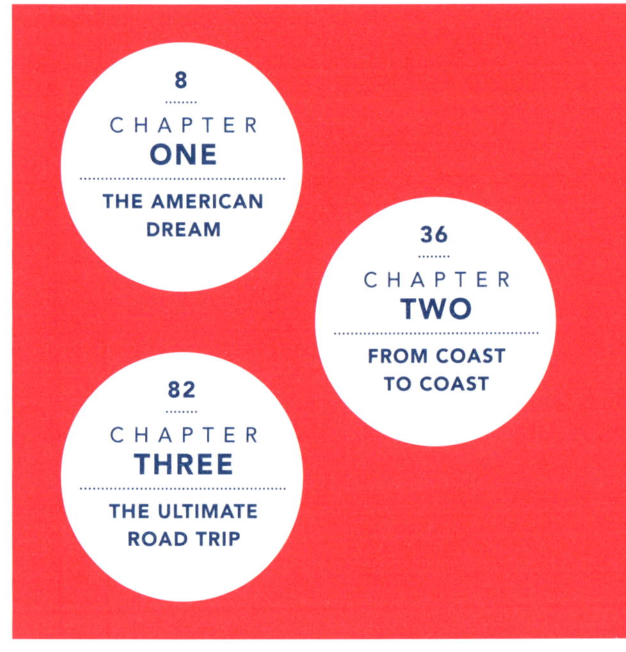

INTRODUCTION

In 2026, the USA celebrates 250 years since its founding. In that time, the country has witnessed more than most could imagine: civil wars, Moon landings, cultural revolutions and pop icons that define generations. From a loose collection of colonies to a global superpower, the USA has grown into a nation whose reach, influence and contradictions are as vast and varied as its landscapes and people.

America is enormous – not only in land, spanning deserts, mountains and endless plains, but in population, diversity and ambition. The country is a mosaic of ideas, cultures and personalities – its contributions to music, literature, science and innovation have shaped the world, while its quirks – oversized diners, offbeat roadside attractions and the occasional improbable invention – give it a unique charm all its own.

This book is a road trip through that complexity. It's a compact guide to the facts, stats, stories and surprises that define the USA, offering insight into what makes the country remarkable, at times paradoxical and endlessly fascinating.

Whether you're stopping to explore an iconic landmark or discovering a hidden oddity, you'll encounter the energy, humour and resilience that have carried America through two and a half centuries.

From coast to coast, and from the well-known to the obscure, this book celebrates the nation's achievements and its enduring spirit. Compact in size but rich in perspective, it's ready to accompany you on your own exploration of a country that continues to surprise, inspire and sometimes confound.

Welcome to the USA – enjoy the journey!

CHAPTER ONE

The phrase "American Dream" was popularized by James Truslow Adams in 1931, yet its ideals reach back to 1776, when the Declaration of Independence proclaimed all men are created equal.

Little did Adams know his words would come to define the hopes of generations of Americans.

THE AMERICAN DREAM

JULY 4, 1776

The date America formally declared its independence from Britain with the adoption of the Declaration of Independence.

It was signed by 56 Founding Fathers. These included its primary author, Thomas Jefferson, as well as Benjamin Franklin, John Adams and John Hancock, the president of the Continental Congress – who signed first with a famously large and bold signature. George Washington did not sign the document, as he was leading the Continental Army in the fight against the British at the time.

“

We hold these truths to be self-evident: that all men are created equal; that they are endowed by their Creator with certain unalienable rights; that among these are Life, Liberty and the pursuit of Happiness.

”

Thomas Jefferson
Declaration of Independence, July 4, 1776

At the time of Christopher Columbus's arrival in the Americas in 1492, it is believed that more than 580 Native American tribes, numbering around eight million people, lived across the continent – each with their own beliefs, rituals and practices.

By 1776, this population had declined by roughly half due to disease, conflict and colonization.

The history of America can be divided into 12 eras:

1. Colonial Settlement (1600s–1763)
2. The American Revolution (1763–1783)
3. The New Nation (1783–1815)
4. National Expansion and Reform (1815–1860)
5. Civil War and Reconstruction (1861–1877)
6. Rise of Industrial America (1877–1900)
7. Progressive Era to New Era (1900–1929)
8. Great Depression and the Second World War (1929–1945)
9. The Post-war US (1945–1968)
10. The Modern Era (1968–present)

OCTOBER 30, 1789

The War of Independence's major fighting effectively ended at Yorktown, Virginia, when British forces surrendered after a three-week siege and heavy losses.

This decisive defeat convinced the British government that it could not win a war fought so far from home.

An iconic oil painting by John Trumbull capturing a key moment of the surrender now hangs in the US Capitol Rotunda.

“

God grant that not only the love of liberty but a thorough knowledge of the rights of man may pervade all the nations of the earth, so that a philosopher may set his foot anywhere on its surface and say, ‘This is my country.’

”

Benjamin Franklin
Letter to David Hartley, December 4, 1789

"

Patriotism is easy to understand in America. It means looking out for yourself by looking out for your country.

"

Calvin Coolidge
"The Destiny of America" speech, May 30, 1923

"Fourscore and seven years ago, our fathers brought forth on this continent, a new nation, conceived in Liberty, and dedicated to the proposition that all men are created equal… This nation, under God, shall have a new birth of freedom, and that government of the people, by the people, for the people, shall not perish from the earth."

Abraham Lincoln
Gettysburg Address, November 19, 1863

Lin-Manuel Miranda's 2015 hit musical *Hamilton* tells the story of Alexander Hamilton – Founding Father, first Secretary of the Treasury and revolutionary leader – charting his rise during the American Revolution and his fateful duel with Aaron Burr. It is one of the highest-grossing Broadway productions in history.

"*Hamilton* is about America then, as told by America now," Miranda said of his creation.

"Let Americans disdain to be the instruments of European greatness! Let the 13 States, bound together in a strict and indissoluble Union, concur in erecting one great American system, superior to the control of all transatlantic force or influence, and able to dictate the terms of the connection between the old and the new world!"

Alexander Hamilton
Federalist No. 11, November 4, 1787

APRIL 30, 1789

The day George Washington took the oath as the first President of the United States.

Unlike his 46 successors, Washington never campaigned and didn't seek the office – he was chosen by popular demand. After the British defeat, many urged him to become king, but he refused, believing in self-governance.

In his Farewell Address (September 19, 1796), he called on citizens to unite beyond themselves: "Citizens by birth or choice, of a common country, that country has a right to concentrate your affections. The name of American… must always exalt the just pride of patriotism."

“I was born an American; I will live an American; I shall die an American!”

Daniel Webster
US Senate speech, March 7, 1850

THE BILL OF RIGHTS

The first 10 amendments to the US Constitution, collectively known as the Bill of Rights, guarantee fundamental rights and freedoms to individuals.

They were ratified on December 15, 1791. Let's remind ourselves what they are:

First Amendment: guarantees freedom of religion, speech, the press, assembly and the right to petition the government.

Second Amendment: protects the right of the people to keep and bear arms.

Third Amendment: prevents the government from forcing citizens to quarter soldiers in their homes during peacetime.

Fourth Amendment: protects against unreasonable searches and seizures of person or property; requires probable cause for warrants.

Fifth Amendment: ensures due process of law, protects against self-incrimination (right to remain

silent) and double jeopardy (being tried twice for the same crime), and guarantees just compensation for private property taken for public use.

Sixth Amendment: guarantees rights to a speedy and public trial, an impartial jury, to be informed of charges, to confront witnesses and to have legal counsel.

Seventh Amendment: provides the right to a jury trial in certain civil cases.

Eighth Amendment: prohibits excessive bail and fines, and cruel and unusual punishments.

Ninth Amendment: states that the enumeration of specific rights in the Constitution does not mean that other rights not listed are not retained by the people.

Tenth Amendment: reserves powers not delegated to the federal government by the Constitution, nor prohibited by it to the states, to the states respectively, or to the people.

"True patriotism springs from a belief in the dignity of the individual, freedom and equality, not only for Americans but for all people on Earth."

Eleanor Roosevelt

Book of Common Sense Etiquette, 1962*

* Roosevelt's legacy as America's longest-serving First Lady endures. She held the position during her husband Franklin D. Roosevelt's four terms as president, from 1933 to 1945. (A two-term limit for presidents was later imposed in 1951.)

JUNETEENTH

June 19, better known as Juneteenth, commemorates the emancipation of enslaved African Americans.

It marks the moment in 1865 when Union soldiers arrived in Galveston, Texas, to announce to the last enslaved people – two years after the Emancipation Proclamation – that they were free.

THE GREATEST AMERICAN

In a 2005 poll of 2.4 million Americans conducted by the Discovery Channel, 40th president Ronald Reagan was voted the greatest American of all time.

His two terms in office (1981–89) are associated with economic prosperity, a period of stability following the bloody Vietnam War and progress towards ending the Cold War.

Before becoming president, Reagan was an actor. He starred in more than 50 Hollywood films, often typecast as the the good guy. His film *Knute Rockne: All American* (1940) is probably his best.

"America is too great for small dreams."

Ronald Reagan
State of the Union address, January 25, 1984

On January 1, 1892 – New Year's Day – a 17-year-old Irish girl named Annie Moore became the first immigrant to be processed at the US federal immigration station on New York's Ellis Island.

She was presented with a $10 gold piece as a symbolic welcome to America.

In its first 62 years of operation, Ellis Island welcomed over 12 million immigrants, and it's estimated that roughly 40 per cent of all Americans can trace some of their ancestry to migrants who passed through Ellis Island.

“

The fact is, with every friendship you make, and every bond of trust you establish, you are shaping the image of America projected to the rest of the world.

”

Michelle Obama,
Young African Leaders Initiative, June 26, 2011

"I pledge allegiance to the Flag of the United States of America, and to the Republic for which it stands, one Nation under God, indivisible, with liberty and justice for all."

The Pledge of Allegiance
Written by Francis Ballamy, 1892

“America was not built on fear. America was built on courage, on imagination and an unbeatable determination to do the job at hand.”

Harry S. Truman,
First Economic Report, January 8, 1947

God bless America, land that I love.
Stand beside her and guide her
Through the night with the light
from above.

From the mountains to
the prairies,
To the oceans white with foam,
God bless America, my home
sweet home,
God bless America, my home
sweet home.

Irving Berlin
"God Bless America", 1918

“When an American says that he loves his country, he means not only that he loves the New England hills, the prairies, glistening in the sun, the wide and rising plains, the great mountains and the sea. He means that he loves an inner air, an inner light in which freedom lives and in which a man can draw the breath of self-respect.”

Adlai Stevenson II

"The Nature of Patriotism", August 27, 1952

AMERICA'S DAD

Actor and all-round nice guy Tom Hanks is affectionately called "America's Dad".

From Woody in the animated *Toy Story* to Captain Sully in *Sully*, and from Forrest Gump in *Forrest Gump* to Mister Rogers in *A Beautiful Day in the Neighbourhood*, Hanks' roles frequently embody the kindness, decency and perseverance associated with America's everyman.

"

America is going to be all right, because we constantly get to tell the whole world who we are. We constantly get to define ourselves as Americans. We do have the greatest country in the world. We may move at a slow pace, but we do have the greatest country in the world, because we are always moving towards a more perfect Union.

"

Tom Hanks
Speech at the Museum of Modern Art (MoMA), New York City, November 15, 2016

CHAPTER TWO

The vastness and beauty of America stretch from the Atlantic to the Pacific. Each region offers its own breathtaking sights and experiences, from towering mountains and rolling plains to dense forests and sparkling rivers.

So pack your curiosity, and let's get moving!

FROM COAST TO COAST

3,794,083

square miles*

America is more than twice the size of the European Union.

Its lowest point is Death Valley in eastern California, which is -282 feet (-86 metres) below sea level. Its highest peak is Denali, Alaska, at 20,310 feet (6,190 metres).

The easternmost point is West Quoddy Head, Maine, and the westernmost point is Cape Wrangell on Attu Island, Alaska.

*9,826,630 square kilometres

JULY 4, 1803

On this day, under President Thomas Jefferson, the US made one of history's greatest real estate deals: the Louisiana Purchase.

For $15 million* – a steal! – America acquired 828,000 square miles (2.14 million square km) from France, effectively doubling the nation's size.

French emperor Napoleon Bonaparte agreed to the sale to fund his Napoleonic Wars, later remarking, "America is a fortunate country. She grows by the follies of our European nations."

*Roughly $550 million in today's money

The US takes its motto, *E pluribus unum* ("Out of many, one"), literally. The country is made up of six distinct regions:

1. New England

Connecticut, Maine, Massachusetts, New Hampshire, Rhode Island and Vermont

2. The Mid-Atlantic

Delaware, Maryland, New Jersey, New York, Pennsylvania and the city of Washington, D.C.

3. The South

Alabama, Arkansas, Florida, Georgia, Kentucky, Louisiana, Mississippi, North Carolina, South Carolina, Tennessee, Virginia and West Virginia

4. The Midwest

Illinois, Indiana, Iowa, Kansas, Michigan, Minnesota, Missouri, Nebraska, North Dakota, Ohio, South Dakota and Wisconsin

5. The Southwest

Arizona, New Mexico, Oklahoma and Texas

6. The West

Alaska, Colorado, California, Hawaii, Idaho, Montana, Nevada, Oregon, Utah, Washington and Wyoming

NATIONAL PARKS

North America's 63 national parks span 84 million acres* of wild landscapes and welcome 330 million visitors every year.

From bison and bald eagles to towering redwoods and grand canyons, these parks are legends of natural beauty.

Each one offers a chance to step into some of the most breathtaking wilderness on Earth.

*34 million square km

IN AMERICA'S NATIONAL PARKS, YOU COULD FIND YOURSELF...

Hiking
Camping
Wildlife watching
Rock climbing
Exploring caves and canyons
Swimming

Kayaking
Canoeing
Rafting
Fishing
Stargazing
Skiing
Snowshoeing

The idea of national parks began with artist George Catlin. In 1832, while travelling the northern Great Plains, he grew alarmed at the destruction of Native American cultures, wildlife and wilderness. However, it wasn't until President Theodore Roosevelt signed the Antiquities Act in 1906 that a national programme took shape.

Forty-four years after President Ulysses S. Grant established Yellowstone as the first national park in 1872, President Woodrow Wilson founded the National Park Service, on August 25, 1916. Part of the US Department of the Interior, it safeguards the country's wilderness and historic treasures.

“

There can be nothing in the world more beautiful than the Yosemite, the groves of the giant sequoias and redwoods, the Canyon of the Colorado, the Canyon of the Yellowstone, the Three Tetons; and our people should see to it that they are preserved for their children and their children's children forever, with their majestic beauty all unmarred.

”

President Theodore Roosevelt
Outdoor Pastimes of an American Hunter, 1905

THE GRAND CANYON

The enduring appeal of this natural masterpiece – and what sets it apart beyond its sheer size – is its timeless beauty.

From the stacked pancake rock strata revealing 1.8-billion-years of geological history to its sacred Native American heritage, the Canyon offers far more than just its breathtaking views.

In many ways, it embodies America itself – big, bold and beautiful.

“There will never be a photograph of the Grand Canyon that can adequately describe its depth, breadth and true beauty.”

Stefanie Payne

In 2007, the Grand Canyon Skywalk was unveiled to the world.

This horseshoe-shaped steel walkway, with its acrophobia-inducing glass-bottomed floor, extends 70 feet (25 metres) beyond the Canyon rim. As terrifying as that sounds, the Skywalk's five layers of 2.5-inch (6.3-cm) thick glass can support the weight of 71 fully loaded 747 aeroplanes – and has never cracked.

One of the first people to walk on it was the original moonwalker, Buzz Aldrin.

The Grand Canyon was – finally – designated a National Park by the US Congress in 1919. To date, only 13 of the 63 US National Parks are UNESCO World Heritage sites:

1. Carlsbad Caverns National Park, New Mexico
2. Olympic National Park, Washington
3. Yellowstone National Park, Wyoming
4. Mammoth Cave National Park, Kentucky
5. Glacier National Park, Montana
6. Redwood National Park, California
7. Mesa Verde National Park, Colorado
8. Hawaii Volcanoes National Park, Hawaii
9. Great Smoky Mountains National Park, Tennessee
10. Glacier Bay National Park, Alaska
11. Grand Canyon National Park, Colorado
12. Yosemite National Park, California
13. Everglades National Park, Florida

The Grand Canyon isn't the only colossal hole in the Arizona Desert.

About 110 miles (177 km) away, lies Meteor Crater – the best-preserved meteorite impact site on Earth.

It was formed 50,000 years ago when a meteor slammed into the landscape, leaving a 3,900-foot (1,200-metre) diameter hole, 560 feet (170 metres) deep.

HIKING TIPS

Research your trip thoroughly, check the weather before you go and don't rely on cellular service or a reliable water supply.

Always check the National Parks website: www.nps.gov

1. Wear sturdy and comfortable footwear and be prepared for weather changes.
2. Take plenty of snacks and water.
3. Take a flashlight, compass and map. You may not be able to rely on GPS or phone signals.
4. Check in with the park ranger before leaving and heed any warnings.
5. Know your physical limits.
6. Stay on designated trails for your safety and also to prevent erosion and damage to vegetation.
7. Respect and stay clear of the wildlife. This is their natural habitat and they will behave accordingly.
8. Follow the countryside code – don't litter and leave no trace behind.

NIAGARA FALLS

The majestic Niagara Falls is one of the world's great spectacles. It may not be the tallest waterfall on Earth, but the sheer volume of water cascading over its cliff edges makes it the most powerful and awe-inspiring.

The American and Bridal Falls lie on the US side, while the Horseshoe Falls are on the Canadian side.

"There is an old saying that you have not seen any falls until you have seen Niagara Falls."

John F. Kennedy
35th US president

Stretching across southern New Mexico, White Sands forms the world's largest gypsum dune field.

The brilliant white dunes cover 275 square miles (712 square km), shaped by wind into shifting ridges and hollows.

Despite the harsh environment, unique plants and animals have adapted to survive in this dazzling, otherworldly landscape.

Beneath the rolling hills of central Kentucky lies Mammoth Cave, the world's longest known cave system.

With more than 426 miles (685 km) of explored passageways, its labyrinth includes vast chambers, narrow tunnels and underground rivers.

Archaeological evidence shows human use for thousands of years.

2,340 MILES*

This is the length of America's most iconic river, the Mississippi – which flows from its source at Lake Itasca in northern Minnesota to the Gulf of Mexico in Louisiana.

Dubbed the Economic Superhighway, the river directly flows through 10 US states: Minnesota, Wisconsin, Iowa, Illinois, Missouri, Kentucky, Tennessee, Arkansas, Mississippi and Louisiana.

It's also known by another name due to its distinct chocolate colour: Big Muddy.

*3,766 km

“Sometimes we'd have that whole river all to ourselves for the longest time. Yonder was the banks and the islands, across the water; and maybe a spark – which was a candle in a cabin window – and sometimes on the water you could see a spark or two – on a raft or a scow, you know; and maybe you could hear a fiddle or a song coming over from one of them crafts. It's lovely to live on a raft.”

Mark Twain
Describing the Mississippi River in
The Adventures of Huckleberry Finn (1884)

REDWOOD NATIONAL PARK

Located in northern California, Redwood National Park is home to the tallest trees on Earth. Towering coast redwoods reach heights of over 350 feet (107 metres), some more than 2,000 years old.

These ancient forests shelter diverse wildlife and preserve ecosystems ranging from rugged coastline to prairies, rivers and oak woodlands.

EVERGLADES NATIONAL PARK

Covering much of southern Florida, the Everglades form a vast subtropical wetland of slow-moving water, sawgrass marshes and mangrove forests.

The unique ecosystem is home to alligators, panthers, manatees and countless bird species. Known as the "River of Grass", it is one of the North America's most distinctive and fragile landscapes.

DEATH VALLEY

Straddling California and Nevada, Death Valley is a land of extremes – the driest, lowest and one of the hottest places on Earth.

Despite Death Valley's scorching heat, some life thrives there – such as creosote bushes, desert pupfish and even bighorn sheep.

134°F*

This staggering temperature was recorded on July 10, 1913, at Furnace Creek in the northern part of Death Valley.

It remains the highest temperature ever reliably measured on Earth.

*56.6 degrees celsius

ROCKY MOUNTAINS

Acquired by the US in the 1803 Louisiana Purchase, the Pike's Peak Gold Rush of 1859 drew miners, ranchers, hunters and homesteaders to the Rockies.

The range, about 76 million years old, stretches some 3,000 miles (4,800 km) across six US states. The high peaks and plains are still home to indigenous peoples, including the Ute, Arapaho and Cheyenne, while nearby regions are associated with the Crow, Apache and others.

YOSEMITE NATIONAL PARK

Located in the Sierra Nevada of California, Yosemite is home to three of the 10 highest waterfalls in the world.

Ribbon Falls, in particular, is nine times taller than Niagara Falls.

Horsetail Falls, on the east side of El Capitan, is famous for appearing to be on fire when it reflects the orange glow of sunset.

YELLOWSTONE NATIONAL PARK

The oldest national park in the US is referred to as the "American Serengeti" because it still supports every native large mammal, including:

Bison	Pronghorn
Elk	Black Bears
Mule Deer	Grizzly Bears
Wolves	Moose
Coyotes	Mountain Lions

Sited on an ancient volcanic caldera, Yellowstone contains the majority of all the geysers in the world.

Boardwalk trails provide easy access to some of the 10,000 hydrothermal features, which include hot springs, fumaroles and mudpots.

Old Faithful,

the most famous geyser, erupts around 20 times a day.

The Great Smoky Mountains – stretching across eastern Tennessee and western North Carolina – rise along the Appalachian chain, their misty peaks covered in ancient forests.

Full of natural wonders, the region showcases Cherokee heritage, early European settler homesteads and the echoes of nineteenth-century logging adventures.

“The United States themselves are essentially the greatest poem.”

Walt Whitman
Preface to *Leaves of Grass*, 1855

The first National Monument, designated in 1906, is Devils Tower in Wyoming.

This geological marvel was formed by cooling magma and rises 1,267 feet (386 metres) above the Belle Fourche River.

Sacred to numerous Native American tribes, who call it Mato Tipila, Devils Tower has been a world-renowned destination for crack climbing since the first known ascent on July 4, 1893, when climbers used a ladder of wooden pegs.

MONUMENT VALLEY

Straddling the Arizona-Utah border, Monument Valley's sandstone buttes – some over 1,000 feet (305 metres) tall – are among the most iconic images of the American West.

Formed by millions of years of erosion, the valley is part of the Navajo Nation and holds deep cultural significance.

Crater Lake, Oregon – the deepest lake in the US – was formed when Mount Mazama collapsed nearly 8,000 years ago.

Its astonishing blue waters are fed only by rain and snow. Visitors explore rim drives, boat tours and Wizard Island – a striking volcanic cinder cone rising from the lake.

“

…but I preferred reading the American landscape as we went along. Every bump, rise and stretch in it mystified my longing.

”

Jack Kerouac
On the Road, 1957

As well as being the largest mammal in North America, the American bison is the national mammal – although this designation was only made official in May 2016.

In the 1800s, there were an estimated 60 million wild bison, but they were hunted to near extinction at the end of that century, when only a few hundred remained.

Today, more than 500,000 roam the continent.

Mount Rushmore, the Black Hills of South Dakota's most famous tourist landmark, features the 60-foot (18.2-metre) faces of Presidents George Washington, Thomas Jefferson, Theodore Roosevelt and Abraham Lincoln.

Conceived by historian Doane Robinson to attract visitors to the Black Hills, it was carved by Gutzon Borglum and his team between 1927 and 1941. Today, more than two million people visit annually.

NEVER FORGET

The 50 states – and their quirky and often surprising nicknames – in alphabetical order:

1. **Alabama:** The Yellowhammer State
2. **Alaska:** The Last Frontier
3. **Arizona:** The Grand Canyon State
4. **Arkansas:** The Natural State
5. **California:** The Golden State
6. **Colorado:** The Centennial State
7. **Connecticut:** The Constitution State
8. **Delaware:** The Diamond State
9. **Florida:** The Sunshine State
10. **Georgia:** The Peach State
11. **Hawaii:** The Aloha State

12. Idaho: The Gem State
13. Illinois: The Prairie State
14. Indiana: The Hoosier State
15. Iowa: The Hawkeye State
16. Kansas: The Sunflower State
17. Kentucky: The Bluegrass State
18. Louisiana: The Pelican State
19. Maine: The Pine Tree State
20. Maryland: The Old Line State
21. Massachusetts: The Bay State
22. Michigan: The Great Lakes State
23. Minnesota: The North Star State
24. Mississippi: The Magnolia State

continued over...

25. Missouri: The Show Me State

26. Montana: The Treasure State

27. Nebraska: The Cornhusker State

28. Nevada: The Silver State

29. New Hampshire: The Granite State

30. New Jersey: The Garden State

31. New Mexico: The Land of Enchantment

32. New York: The Empire State

33. North Carolina: The Tar Heel State

34. North Dakota: The Peace Garden State

35. Ohio: The Buckeye State

36. Oklahoma: The Sooner State

37. Oregon: The Beaver State

38. Pennsylvania: The Keystone State

39. Rhode Island: The Ocean State

40. South Carolina: The Palmetto State

41. South Dakota: The Mount Rushmore State
(replacing the nickname The Coyote State in 1980)

42. Tennessee: The Volunteer State

43. Texas: The Lone Star State

44. Utah: The Beehive State

45. Vermont: The Green Mountain State

46. Virginia: The Old Dominion

47. Washington: The Evergreen State

48. West Virginia: The Mountain State

49. Wisconsin: The Badger State

50. Wyoming: The Cowboy State

663,268

square miles*

The total area of Alaska, by far the largest state in the US.

Alaska is more than twice the size of the second-largest state, Texas, and bigger than the next three largest (Texas, California and Montana) combined.

* 1,717,856 square km

The smallest state is Rhode Island, with a total area of 1,545 square miles (4,003 square km).

DENALI NATIONAL PARK

Located in Alaska's Denali Borough, this park spans six million acres (about 24,280 square km) of wilderness, bisected by a single 92-mile (148-km) ribbon road.

Home to Denali (formerly Mount McKinley) – North America's tallest peak at 20,310 feet (6,190 metres) – the area is a magnet for mountaineering, skiing and adventure seekers.

In 2019, Hyperion, a coast redwood in California, was officially designated the world's tallest known living tree.

Standing 380.8 feet (116.07 metres) tall, it is believed to be 800 years old.

O beautiful for spacious skies,
For amber waves of grain,
For purple mountain majesties
Above the fruited plain!
America! America!
God shed His grace on thee
And crown thy good with brotherhood
From sea to shining sea!

"America the Beautiful"*

Lyrics by Katharine Lee Bates, music by Samuel A. Ward (1895)

* The two great composers of this anthem, Bates and Ward, never met.

CHAPTER THREE

Americans have always cherished the freedom of the open road. Iconic routes like Route 66 and the Pacific Coast Highway pass through small towns, deserts and bustling cities – each stop offering its own unique sights.

So start your engines, and let the adventure begin!

THE ULTIMATE ROAD TRIP

Stretching 2,448 miles (3,940 km), from Illinois' Land of Lincoln to California's Wild West (and everything in between), Route 66 is synonymous with adventure, freedom and the American Dream.

With breathtaking vistas, motels, drive-ins and neon signs, it remains a pilgrimage for millions of travellers and adventure-seekers.

286 MILLION

The number of cars on American roads.

This is approximately one for every person in the US who is over 16 years old, the legal driving age.

ROUTE 66 WILDLIFE

Route 66 winds through America's diverse landscapes – prairies, deserts, mountains and forests.

As you travel through the highway's eight states, why not try spotting some of the great mammals that call these regions home?

1 Arizona:
Ring-tailed Cat

2 New Mexico:
Black Bear

3 California:
Grizzly Bear

4 Illinois:
White-tailed Deer

5 Kansas:
Bison

6 Missouri:
Missouri Mule

7 Oklahoma:
Buffalo

8 Texas:
Armadillo

MADE OF ROADS

Today, the US boasts the world's largest road network, with a total length of approximately 4.1 million miles (6.6 million km).

The nation's highways connect all 50 states and include some of the world's longest transcontinental routes, such as Interstate 80, Interstate 90, Route 6 and Route 20.

Route 66, America's "Mother Road", became a vital artery for Dust Bowl migrants in the 1930s and a symbol of post-war road trips in the 1950s, lined with quirky roadside attractions.

Although decommissioned in 1985 due to the Interstate Highway System, sections remain preserved as "Historic Route 66", drawing tourists seeking a nostalgic journey.

Its cultural impact is immense, immortalized in songs and literature, truly representing the "Main Street of America".

AMERICA PLAYLIST #1

"Kids in America" – Kim Wilde

"Breakfast in America" – Supertramp

"American Idiot" – Green Day

"American Dream" – MKTO

"Made in America" – Toby Keith

"R.O.C.K. in the USA" – John Mellencamp

"All-American Girl" – Carrie Underwood

"American Kids" – Kenny Chesney

"American Saturday Night"– Brad Paisley

"American Beauty/American Psycho" – Fall Out Boy

Once a must-stop along Route 66, Tucumcari, New Mexico, proudly advertised "Tucumcari Tonight!" on billboards hundreds of miles away, luring weary travellers with promises of rest.

At its peak, the town offered more than 2,000 motel rooms, glowing neon signs and classic diners. Today, many vintage motels and murals still celebrate its roadside heritage.

The world's first drive-thru restaurant – the unbeatable combo of car and fast food – is believed to have started in 1947 at the legendary Red's Giant Hamburg in Springfield, Missouri.

Its infamous roadside sign, a towering cross reading "Giant Hamburg", became iconic before the restraurant finally closed its doors in 1984.

365 HOURS

The time an average American spends in their car – roughly seven hours per week or one hour per day. Of that time, around 54 hours are lost sitting in traffic.

Today, the average American drives approximately 13,700 miles (22,048 km) annually, among the highest per-capita mileages in US history.

On December 5, 1848, President James Polk made a stunning revelation in his State of the Union address – gold flakes had been found at Sutter's Mill, California. Polk's announcement triggered the largest mass migration in American history.

Over the next six years, more than 300,000 people made the 3,000-mile (4,800-km) journey west in the hope of making a fortune.

Overnight, the "Gold Rush" doubled California's population – and the state has never been the same since.

The world's first motorist hotel – or "motel" – was the Motel Inn, in San Luis Obispo, California. It opened on December 12, 1925.

Its location was chosen because San Luis Obispo sits roughly at the midpoint between Los Angeles and San Francisco, then a two-day drive on dirt roads. The concept proved wildly successful – and by 1961, America boasted more than 60,000 motels.

As Hanya Yanagihara once said, "There is something uniquely American about the motel. It speaks to the transient nature of America itself."

“I love everything about motels. I can’t help myself. I still get excited every time I slip a key into a motel room door and fling it open.”

Bill Bryson
Travel writer

8 ICONIC ROUTES

1. **Pacific Coast Highway** (California State Route 1) – San Francisco to Los Angeles
2. **Blue Ridge Parkway** – Virginia to North Carolina
3. **Overseas Highway** (US Route 1, Florida Keys) – Mainland Florida to Key West, FL
4. **Great River Road** – Follows the Mississippi River through 10 states
5. **Lincoln Highway** – Times Square, NY to San Francisco, CA
6. **US Route 20** – Boston, MA to Newport, OR
7. **Natchez Trace Parkway** – Natchez, MS to Nashville, TN
8. **Beartooth Highway** (US 212) – Montana to Wyoming

The US is famed for its weird and wonderful roadside attractions.

A standout is the world's largest ball of twine, near Cawker City, Kansas. Weighing more than 13 tons, it contains an estimated 1,600 miles (2,575 km) of twine!

You don't need to know why it's there...

AMERICA PLAYLIST #2

"An American Trilogy" – Elvis Presley

"America" – Simon & Garfunkel

"Living in America" – James Brown

"God Bless the USA" – Lee Greenwood

"This Is America" – Childish Gambino

"American Pie" – Don McLean

"Born in the USA" – Bruce Springsteen

"Young Americans" – David Bowie

"Party in the USA" – Miley Cyrus

"American Girl" – Tom Petty and the Heartbreakers

“There is no place, no country, more compassionate, more generous, more accepting and more welcoming than the United States of America.”

Arnold Schwarzenegger
Address to the Republican National Convention,
August 31, 2004

An icon of the Beat generation, Jack Kerouac immortalized the American road in his novel *On the Road*, capturing the restless spirit of a generation seeking freedom and adventure.

For Kerouac, the open highway is a symbol of possibility, rebellion and exploration.

“Nothing behind me, everything ahead of me, as is ever so on the road.”

Jack Kerouac
On the Road, 1957

CHAPTER FOUR

Americans have always been drawn to the energy of their cities. From the skyscrapers of New York and Chicago to the music-filled streets of New Orleans and Nashville, each city has its own rhythm and flavour.

So grab a map, and let's hit the streets!

CITY LIGHTS

6 CITY NICKNAMES

America's cities are full of personality, and many have earned quirky nicknames:

New York
The Big Apple

Chicago
The Windy City

New Orleans
The Big Easy

Seattle
The Emerald City

Denver
Mile-High City

San Francisco
The Golden City

19,430

The approximate number of incorporated cities, towns and villages in the US – each brimming with its own unique culture and history.

From Broadway lights in New York and blues clubs in Chicago to sleepy main streets in small towns across the Midwest and South, every city has its quirks, landmarks and local traditions.

THE BIG APPLE

New York City is one of the world's most visited cities. On first impression, it's loud, busy and expensive, but still – there's something uniquely special about it.

Each neighbourhood has its own particular vibe – a melting pot of different cultures that brings with it a diversity of offerings.

New York has something for everyone.

NYC BUSES

On an average weekday, New York City buses carry 2.2 million people.

With over 675 million rides a year, NYC buses carry more passengers than the next three largest city bus systems combined – those of Los Angeles, Chicago and San Francisco.

"When I was growing up, I don't remember being told that America was created so that everyone could get rich. I remember being told it was about opportunity and the pursuit of happiness. Not happiness itself, but the pursuit."

Martin Scorsese
Interview with *The Independent*,
December 13, 2013

50,000

The number of bats living in Austin, Texas – home to the world's largest urban bat colony.

Each spring, Mexican free-tailed bats take up residence under the city's Congress Avenue Bridge.

From spring through early autumn, thousands of spectators gather nightly to watch the bats form a mesmerizing spectacle across the twilight sky.

San Francisco's Chinatown, founded in 1848, is the oldest in North America and still the largest outside Asia. Beyond its dragon gates lie bustling markets, herbal shops, temples and dim sum eateries.

Rich in tradition and history, it remains one of the city's most vibrant and colourful neighbourhoods.

“We are a nation of many nationalities, many races, many religions – bound together by a single unity, the unity of freedom and equality.”

Franklin D. Roosevelt
Campaign address, November 1, 1940

38.6 MILLION

The number of books in the Library of Congress in Washington, DC, the world's largest library.

If stacked vertically, the books would reach about 762 miles (1,225 km) high, roughly equivalent to the east–west length of Texas.

Many American cities hide underground passages, tunnels and catacombs.

In Seattle, floods and fires led to a mysterious underground city; Portland boasts the legendary Prohibition-era Shanghai Tunnels; and Houston hosts climate-controlled pedestrian tunnels connecting downtown blocks.

“

One flag, one land, one heart, one hand, one nation, evermore!

”

Oliver Wendell Holmes, Sr
"Voyage of the United States Frigate Constitution",
1894

LAS VEGAS

Described by Hunter S. Thompson as the "savage heart of the American Dream", there's nowhere else on Earth quite like Nevada's Las Vegas – the "Gambling Capital of America". Each year, the 64 casinos on the Strip rake in more than $10 billion in profit.

As David Hickey once said, "America is a very poor lens through which to view Las Vegas, while Las Vegas is a wonderful lens through which to view America."

10 CITY LANDMARKS

1. **New York, NY** – Statue of Liberty
2. **Washington, DC** – Lincoln Memorial
3. **San Francisco, CA** – Golden Gate Bridge
4. **Chicago, IL** – Willis Tower
5. **Las Vegas, NV** – The Strip
6. **New Orleans, LA** – St Louis Cathedral
7. **Philadelphia, PA** – Liberty Bell
8. **Boston, MA** – Freedom Trail
9. **Los Angeles, CA** – Hollywood Sign
10. **Seattle, WA** – Space Needle

Gifted by France in 1886 to celebrate friendship, the Statue of Liberty became a beacon of hope for immigrants arriving in New York.

A bronze plaque at its base features Emma Lazarus's 1883 poem, "A New Colossus", with the famous lines, "Give me your tired, your poor… I lift my lamp beside the golden door!"

ALL THAT JAZZ

A truly American art form, jazz emerged as the sound of the country's cultural renaissance in the 1920s.

Its origins lie deep within the African-American communities of late nineteenth-century New Orleans, where blues, ragtime, spirituals and brass band music blended to create a new sound.

Louis Armstrong, affectionately nicknamed "Satchmo" and born in poverty in New Orleans, became jazz's first global superstar.

More than 300 languages are spoken across the US, with over 80 languages heard in New York City alone.

The country has no official language, but English is the most widely spoken, used by 78.2 per cent of the population, followed by Spanish at 13 per cent.

CITY MAGNETS

The US welcome millions of international visitors each year, offering iconic landmarks, cultural highlights and unforgettable experiences.

Here are the eight most-visited cities:

1. New York City:
8.89 million

2. Miami:
4.37 million

3. Los Angeles:
3.6 million

4. Orlando:
3.52 million

5. San Francisco:
2.28 million

6. Las Vegas:
2.08 million

7. Washington, DC:
1.61 million

8. Chicago:
1.41 million

While the US may no longer hold the record for the most skyscrapers – that title goes to China – it does boast the world's first skyscraper. And no, it wasn't in New York.

The first building to surpass 492 feet (150 metres), today's standard for a skyscraper, was Philadelphia City Hall, completed in 1894.

Tucked into the heart of Portland, Oregon, Forest Park – the largest urban forest in the US – stretches around eight square miles (21 square km).

With more than 80 miles (129 km) of winding trails, towering trees and hidden wildlife, it's a place where city sounds fade and nature takes over.

"Within the soul of America is freedom of mind and spirit in man. Here alone are the open windows through which pours the sunlight of the human spirit."

Herbert Hoover
In a speech titled "The Meaning of America", August 10, 1948

CHAPTER FIVE

From the jazz clubs of New Orleans to Hollywood films, bestselling blockbusters and groundbreaking art, America's culture is as diverse as its people.

So tune in, turn the page and let's explore the creativity that makes the country unique!

STARS AND STRIPES

The US is credited as the birthplace of rock and roll.

In the 1930s and 1940s, Sister Rosetta Tharpe – often called the "Godmother of Rock and Roll" – brought energetic guitar-driven gospel music that directly influenced early rock artists such as Chuck Berry, Little Richard and Bill Haley.

Tharpe famously reflected, "Oh, these kids and rock and roll – that is just sped-up rhythm and blues. I've been doing that forever!"

The "King of Rock and Roll", Elvis Presley, remains the ultimate American idol. A symbol of the American Dream, he rose from humble beginnings to sell over one billion records – making him the best-selling solo artist in history.

Elvis never toured abroad. He left the country only during his US Army service in Germany.

AMERICAN AS APPLE PIE

Apple pie is America's quintessential sweet symbol of home and tradition.

Warm, cinnamon-spiced apples nestled in flaky, buttery crust evoke cozy family gatherings and holiday celebrations.

Whether enjoyed cold with a scoop of vanilla ice cream or fresh from the oven, apple pie remains a beloved centrepiece at family tables nationwide.

“

I’m more American than apple pie. I’m like apple pie, with a hot dog in it.

”

Stephen Colbert
Comedian and writer

BASEBALL

Part sport, part cultural heartbeat, baseball holds a special place in American life.

Generations bond over shared traditions, box scores and rivalries. From small-town diamonds to grand stadiums, it brings people together with a shared love for the crack of the bat – and a good hot dog.

“I see great things in baseball. It’s our game – the American game.”

Walt Whitman
Poet and journalist

Martin Luther King Jr's "I Have a Dream" speech – delivered to more than 250,000 supporters from the steps of the Lincoln Memorial on August 28, 1963 – endures as America's most famous public address.

The speech's iconic refrain was improvised on the spot, a departure from King's prepared remarks that became one of the most celebrated ad-lib moments in US history.

“I say to you today, my friends, that in spite of the difficulties and frustrations of the moment, I still have a dream.

Martin Luther King Jr
"I Have a Dream" speech, August 28, 1963

SUPERBOWL

It's Superbowl Sunday – the second Sunday in February and one of the biggest days in American sports. Nearly half the nation tunes in – roughly 128 million people – to watch the annual championship game for American football.

The Halftime Show has become a star in its own right. For Super Bowl LIX in 2025, Kendrick Lamar's performance drew 133.5 million viewers – the most-watched TV concert in history.

Peanut butter and jelly* – or PB&J – is a favourite lunch option, especially among children.

Every April 2, millions of Americans celebrate National Peanut Butter and Jelly Day, marking the fact that the average citizen will eat more than 2,000 PB&Js by the time they graduate from high school – and more than 3,000 in their lifetime.

That's roughly one every 10 days!

* Or jam, as it's known elsewhere.

1:59.40

The record-breaking time Secretariat set in 1973 to win the Kentucky Derby at Churchill Downs in Louisville – the nation's longest-running annual sporting event.

He was the first horse in Derby history to break the two-minute mark. Nicknamed "The Run for the Roses", the Derby is the crown jewel of horse racing's Triple Crown, alongside the Preakness Stakes and the Belmont Stakes.

If you've ever wondered about the origins of country music, look no further than Bristol, Tennessee – formally recognized by Congress in 1988 as the "Birthplace of Country Music".

The historic 1927 Bristol Sessions, featuring pioneers like the Carter Family and Jimmie Rodgers, are often called the "Big Bang" of country music.

O say can you see, by the dawn's early light,
What so proudly we hailed at the twilight's
last gleaming,
Whose broad stripes and bright stars
through the perilous fight
O'er the ramparts we watched were so
gallantly streaming?
And the rocket's red glare, the bomb
bursting in air,
Gave proof through the night that our flag
was still there,
O say does that star-spangled banner
yet wave
O'er the land of the free and the home of
the brave?

"The Star-Spangled Banner", written by Francis Scott Key in 1814, was inspired by the sight of the American flag still flying over Fort McHenry after a night of British bombardment in the War of 1812.

Originally a poem titled "Defense of Fort M'Henry" and set to the tune of a British drinking song, it became the US national anthem in 1931.

Today, its first verse is sung before nearly every major sporting event.

“After all, tomorrow is another day!”

Scarlett O' Hara
The heroine's classic line from
Margaret Mitchell's Pulitzer Prize-winning novel
Gone With the Wind, 1936

The term "Great American Novel", coined by John William De Forest in an 1868 essay, refers to a book that embodies and examines the essence and character of the US. Some of the top candidates include:

1. *The Adventures of Huckleberry Finn* – Mark Twain (1884)
2. *Moby-Dick* – Herman Melville (1851)
3. *The Great Gatsby* – F. Scott Fitzgerald (1925)
4. *The Grapes of Wrath* – John Steinbeck (1939)
5. *To Kill a Mockingbird* – Harper Lee (1960)
6. *Invisible Man* – Ralph Ellison (1952)
7. *The Catcher in the Rye* – J.D. Salinger (1951)
8. *Beloved* – Toni Morrison (1987)
9. *Catch-22* – Joseph Heller (1961)
10. *Slaughterhouse-Five* – Kurt Vonnegut (1969)

THANKSGIVING

Celebrated on the fourth Thursday in November, Thanksgiving is a uniquely American tradition. It traces back to the 1621 harvest feast shared by 50 Plymouth colonists and 90 Wampanoag people, giving thanks for a successful harvest.

Today, 46 million turkeys are cooked annually – but two are always spared. In 1989, President George H.W. Bush began the tradition of pardoning a turkey, allowing it to live out a full and adventurous life.

In 1924, 16-year-old short-order cook Lionel Sternberger was working at his father's sandwich shop, The Rite Spot, in Pasadena, California, when he accidentally invented the cheeseburger.

He dropped a slice of American cheese on a sizzling hamburger – and the rest, as they say, is history…

INDEPENDENCE DAY

This celebrated day on July 4 marks the adoption of the Declaration of Independence in 1776.

Families gather for barbecues, parades and spectacular fireworks.

3 BILLION

The number of pizzas* that are sold in the US each year.

Americans consume roughly 100 acres (41 hectares) of pizza each day – about 350 slices per second.

*The nation's favourite topping? Pepperoni.

American basketball began in December 1891, invented by James Naismith in Springfield, Massachusetts. It quickly spread through colleges and became professional with the formation of the NBA in 1949.

One of the most famous NBA moments is Michael Jordan's "The Shot" in the 1989 playoffs between the Chicago Bulls and Cleveland Cavaliers – a game-winning jumper with three seconds left to give the Bulls a 101–100 victory.

TEDDY BEAR

This soft toy is named after President Theodore "Teddy" Roosevelt. Its origin dates back to a 1902 Mississippi bear hunt, when Roosevelt refused to shoot a tied-up bear, calling it unsportsmanlike.

The *Washington Post* immortalized the moment in a cartoon, inspiring Brooklyn candy shop owner Morris Michtom to create and sell stuffed "Teddy's Bears".

The Met, located in New York City, is the largest art museum in the US and one of the most comprehensive in the world.

Housing more than two million works of art, it spans 5,000 years of human history – from ancient Egyptian artefacts and classical sculptures to European masterpieces and modern American art.

Once dismissed as mere vandalism, graffiti has become a celebrated part of American culture.

Colourful murals, spray-painted designs and hip-hop-inspired creations now brighten galleries like Miami's Museum of Graffiti – proving that street art is a dynamic, uniquely American way to make a statement.

HOLLYWOOD

In the 1910s, Hollywood became the epicentre of American film.

From silent movies to modern blockbusters, it's where stars are born and dreams are made.

Each year, millions of visitors flock to see the glitz, take selfies with iconic signs and experience a bit of movie magic firsthand.

Orson Welles's 1941 masterpiece *Citizen Kane* remains a landmark of American cinema.

Written and directed by Welles – who also stars in the film – it redefined filmmaking by exploring the complex life of publishing magnate Charles Foster Kane.

With its themes of power, ambition and corruption, it consistently ranks as the number-one movie on the American Film Institute's Top 100 list.

“

People say that if you don’t love America, then get the hell out. Well, I love America.

”

Ron Kovic (Tom Cruise)
Born on the Fourth of July, 1989

$10 BILLION

The amount Americans spend each year on treats, costumes and decorations to celebrate Halloween, on October 31.

From trick-or-treating to pumpkin carving, it's the country's spookiest and most fun-filled holiday.

“

I’m here to fight for truth and justice, and the American Way.

”

Superman (Christopher Reeves)
Superman, 1978

Created in 1938 by Jerry Siegel and Joe Shuster, Superman is considered the first major superhero and helped launch the golden age of American comics.

His red cape, blue suit and "S" emblem have become enduring symbols of heroism and American pop culture.

JUNE 14 - FLAG DAY

This day honours the adoption of the US flag. Its 13 red and white stripes represent the original colonies: Delaware, Pennsylvania, New Jersey, Georgia, Connecticut, Massachusetts, Maryland, South Carolina, New Hampshire, Virginia, New York, North Carolina and Rhode Island.

Each of the colours on the flag has a meaning:

Red: valour and bravery
White: purity and innocence
Blue: vigilance, perseverance and justice

The Minnesota State Fair is the largest in the US, attracting over two million visitors in just 12 days each August.

Known as "The Great Minnesota Get-Together", it's a carnival of food, music, rides and quirky competitions – from giant vegetable contests to butter sculpting.

THE LAST MONDAY OF MAY

Often considered the unofficial start of summer, Memorial Day honours the millions of soldiers who died serving in the US armed forces.

“

This nation will remain the land of the free only so long as it is the home of the brave.

”

Elmer Davis

Director of the Office of War Information during the Second World War

The blues originated in the Deep South, emerging from the work songs, spirituals and chants of enslaved and newly freed Black Americans after the Civil War.

The first blues recording is widely considered to be "Crazy Blues" by Mamie Smith, released in 1920.

“The blues are the roots and the other musics are the fruits. It’s better keeping the roots alive, because it means better fruits from now on. As long as American music survives, so will the blues.”

Willie Dixon
Pivotal figure in shaping the Chicago blues sound

Americans drink roughly 400 million cups of coffee every day, more than any other nation per capita.

From quick morning pick-me-ups to leisurely cafe visits, coffee is an essential part of daily life.

6.3 BILLION GALLONS*

The amount of beer Americans consume each year.

From craft breweries popping up in every state to iconic brands, beer is a staple at barbecues, sporting events and social gatherings.

*23.8 billion litres

On February 22, 1980, at the Winter Olympics in Lake Placid, New York, the US Men's Olympic Ice Hockey Team – an underdog squad of amateur and college players – pulled off one of sports' greatest upsets by defeating the mighty Soviet Union, four-time defending gold medallists.

The team went on to win gold by beating Finland.

“

Do you believe in miracles? Yes!

”

Al Michael

Commentator during the US vs Soviet Union ice hockey game at the 1980 Winter Olympics

CHAPTER SIX

From fabulous inventions to jaw-dropping feats, America does things big. From the first powered flight to the largest hamburger, the country is full of one-of-a-kinds.

So buckle up, because we're about to explore the quirks, firsts and feats that make the US unlike anywhere else.

BORN IN THE USA

69 PER CENT*

The share of Americans who believe it is the character of the American people that is the essential key to the country's success.

*Pew Research Center

GROUNDHOG DAY

One of America's quirkiest traditions is Groundhog Day, celebrated every February 2.

According to legend, if a groundhog named Punxsutawney Phil emerges from his burrow at Gobbler's Knob, Pennsylvania, and sees his shadow, it predicts six more weeks of winter.

Since Phil's first recorded prediction in 1887, he's been correct only about 39 per cent of the time.

The US is full of towns with quirky, strange or downright confusing names. Here are 10 of the best:

1. Boring, OR

Officially paired with Dull, Scotland.

2. Truth or Consequences, NM

Named after a 1950s radio show.

3. Chicken, AK

Chosen because early residents struggled to spell "Ptarmigan".

4. Intercourse, PA

A popular Amish country town with a cheeky name.

5. Nameless, TN

Residents couldn't agree on a name…

6. Monkey's Eyebrow, KY

Well, why not?

7. Nothing, AZ

Ghost town with a population of zero.

8. Santa Claus, GA

Embraces the festive spirit year round.

9. Odd, WV

Locals wanted an "odd" name.

10. Hot Coffee, MS

Named after a popular inn.

66 PER CENT

The percentage of Americans – about 87 million households – that have at least one pet.

Dogs rule the roost, with an estimated 89.7 million calling the US home.

As of May 2025, the most popular dog names were Luna and Charlie.

162 MILLION

The number of bottles of Jack Daniel's sold worldwide each year. It has been the best-selling American whiskey since it was created in 1866 in Lynchburg, Tennessee, at the oldest registered US distillery.

Frank Sinatra loved it so much that he wanted to be buried with a bottle – so his daughter Nancy slipped one into his coffin.

With his white top hat, blue jacket and red bow tie, Uncle Sam has personified the US since the War of 1812.

The nickname is said to come from Samuel Wilson, a meat packer who supplied barrels stamped "US" to soldiers.

In 1917, artist J. M. Flagg created the iconic "I Want YOU for US Army" poster, later used in both world wars to recruit soldiers.

97 PER CENT

The percentage of American homes that have a bottle of Heinz Ketchup, the nation's number-one condiment.

The brand, based in Pittsburgh, Pennsylvania, was founded in 1869 and now sells more than 650 million bottles annually worldwide.

On average, Americans consume around 11 lbs (5 kg) of ketchup per person annually.

In 1903, Orville and Wilbur Wright made history at Kitty Hawk, North Carolina, with the first successful powered flight.

Their aircraft stayed aloft for just 12 seconds, but it changed the world forever – and launched America's love affair with aviation.

"The desire to fly is an idea handed down to us by our ancestors who… looked enviously on the birds soaring freely through space… on the infinite highway of the air."

Wilbur Wright
Letter to the Aéro Club de France, November 5, 1908

On July 21, 1969, Neil Armstrong became the first person to set foot on the Moon – an historic moment celebrated around the world.

It was America's scientific might and $25 billion investment (about $200 billion today) that made it possible.

In the years since, only 12 people – all Americans – have walked on the lunar surface.

“That’s one small step for man, one giant leap for mankind.”

Neil Armstrong
First person to walk on the Moon, 1969

15 BILLION

The number of bushels of corn the US produces each year, making it the world's largest producer.

Most grows in the Corn Belt – Iowa, Illinois, Indiana, Ohio, Nebraska, Kansas, Missouri and Minnesota.

Popcorn is America's oldest snack – Native Americans were popping corn long before Europeans arrived.

Today, Americans eat roughly 17 billion quarts (9.7 billion kg) of it each year.

AUGUST 2, 2018

The date that Apple, based in California, became the world's first publicly traded company to reach a $1 trillion market value – a milestone driven by strong sales of iPhones, Macs and other products since 2007.

Today, other tech giants – including Microsoft, Amazon, Alphabet, Meta Platforms and Tesla – have also joined the "Trillion Dollar Club".

338 MILLION*

America's population in July 2025.

That's roughly the same as the number of bubbles in a pint of Guinness – America's most popular imported beer.

By 2100, the population is projected to exceed 420 million.

*The US Census Bureau

The first electronic general-purpose computer, ENIAC, was built in 1945 at the University of Pennsylvania.

Weighing 27 tonnes and filling a large room, it could perform 5,000 calculations per second – pretty fast for its time!

This invention laid the foundation for the digital age and America's tech revolution.

WWW.

America is the birthplace of the Internet.

In 1969, ARPANET connected computers at UCLA and Stanford for the first time. Just two years later, Ray Tomlinson sent history's first email – between two side-by-side machines – simply reading, QWERTYUIOP.

It marked the start of the digital revolution that would change the world.

20 BILLION

The number of hot dogs eaten by Americans annually, according to the National Hot Dog and Sausage Council (2025).

That's about 60 per person – with the biggest bite taken between Memorial Day and Labor Day.

On July 4 alone, Americans consume around 150 million hot dogs.

After the Revolutionary War, prominent lexicographer Noah Webster wanted to make American English distinct.

In 1806, he published the first American dictionary, simplifying spellings – "color" instead of "colour," "honor" instead of "honour", and "center" instead of "centre".

Some ideas didn't stick, though – such as "wimmen" for "women"!

$453.60*

The approximate amount the average American spends on tips each year.

A 2024 survey found that the average person "reluctantly" tips $37.80 (£27.85) per month, feeling the pressure of wanting to be seen as a good tipper.

*£334.20

9,982

The number of calories* in the infamous “Quadruple Bypass Burger”, served at Las Vegas’s Heart Attack Grill.

Here, waitresses dressed as uniformed “nurses” take orders written like prescriptions, diners don hospital gowns and anyone over 350 lbs (159 kg) eats for free.

Fail to finish your meal, and the nurses might administer a paddle-spanking.

Only in America!

*Five times more than a man’s recommended daily allowance.

CHARGOGGAGO-GGMANCHAUGG-AGOGGCHAUBU-NAGUNGAMAUGG

This 45-letter mouthful is the longest single-word place name in the US.

It's a lake in Webster, Massachusetts, and comes from the Nipmuc language. The name means "Fishing Place at the Boundaries – Neutral Meeting Grounds".

Unsurprisingly, locals just call it Webster Lake.

America's oldest pub is the White Horse Tavern. Situated on the corner of Farewell and Marlborough streets in Newport, Rhode Island, it has welcomed drinkers and diners since 1673 – long before America was a nation.

If you visit, don't miss the clam chowder!

"

America is another name for opportunity.

"

Ralph Waldo Emerson,
The Conduct of Life, 1860